Marrow of Summer

Marrow of Summer

Poems by

Andrea Potos

Cover design by Shay Culligan

ISBN: 978-1-954353-12-1

Kelsay Books
502 South 1040 East, A-119
American Fork, Utah, 84003

For all the beloveds, gone on

Acknowledgments

Much gratitude to the following publications who first published these poems, sometimes in slightly different form:

Poetry East, Cave Wall, Christian Century, Spirituality & Health, One Art, Bearings Online, Innisfree Poetry Journal, Buddhist Poetry Review, The Aurorean, Headstuff, Braided Way, Orchards Poetry Journal, Peacock Journal, Heron Tree, Hummingbird, Spillway, Sunlight Press, The Blue Nib, gratefulness.org, How to Love the World: Poems of Gratitude and Hope (Storey Publishing).

Gratitude also to those dear people who have supported me and believed in my work through all these years of poetry: Michael Slater, Trish Vanderhoef, Rosemary Zurlo-Cuva, Katrin Talbot and Evie Robillard.

And many thanks to Karen Kelsay and her remarkable staff.

Contents

Summer afternoon—summer afternoon; to me those have always been the two most beautiful words in the English language.

—Henry James

*Do not tell
the world
your pain.*

*Show it
the joy
of your tears.*

—Charles Ghigna

Before Waking in May

There they are, as if on the stillest pond surface:
your crumpled griefs and nibbling fears,
scenes of the ways you have disappointed yourself,
friendship threads frayed or dissolved.
Yet still, you fold aside the blankets,
fluff your pillows and get up.
There's no mistaking the resident cardinals
shouting at you through the window screen.
When you raise the shades,
you notice the emerged leaves of late May;
they have only deepened
their green after rain.

Creating

I think of my Yaya, all those hours
at her Singer sewing machine,
or sitting with her skeins of yarn,
or the thimble on her finger as she
basted and lined
the pleats of the drapes,
the hems of the dresses and skirts and coats,
as she embroidered the doilies and linens,
the pillowcases and sheets.

All I have are my pens, scatterings
of dark blue or black, sometimes purple
or green, depending on the mood,
hoping my hand aligns somehow with hers as
I make small stitches of words across paper
that, sometimes, feels like rough cotton,
sometimes like silk.

In a Midwestern Summer

This morning I am pondering the *grass is always greener*
notion that humans have:
all through the bone-cold January grind,
and the frozen eternity of February we long for
this High Summer, mid-July and all.

I am thinking of this as the damp
thickened cloth of air lays
itself down on my skin, as invisible thumbs
press in at my temples.
Just now I had to quickly commit murder—
a descending bug that sought
to live off a few drops
of my hot blood.

Words and Numbers

I remember my friend, diagnosed
with a brain tumor late last year—
the numbers thrust on him:
12-18 months with treatment,
the highly-praised, high-wired oncologist
blurting his gospel truth:
This thing will get you—
words as explanation, incantation
or harm, I don't know which,
and the ominous assumptions of numbers.
I prayed my friend
wouldn't attach himself to them.
I worried about the destiny of words:
In the beginning was the word after all—
and look at all that burst forth from it.

Wig Shopping With Mom

Though after five months of chemo, her hair
was only thinned a little,
she had a free wig coming,
the nurse told us. We visited the room
of floor-to-ceiling shelves: mannequin
heads, and baskets of scarves and wraps.
Mom settled in; we giggled, comparing
thoughts as she smiled for my cellphone camera:
dark auburn with short curls, layered
brunette waves, medium shaggy, sideways parts;
one wig with streaks of silver like surprise hints of lightning.
In no rush to agree on the one and decide,
we wanted to stay in that brief clearing
of complimentary joy. We never even considered
choosing anything other than hope.

For the Robin on My Porch

How lucky for me that my lampbox ledge
became your chosen landing.
Hour by hour I witnessed
your skills—diving and swooping under the eave
with supplies gleaned from early
spring earth and winter dregs.

You made it look so seamless: circles of twig
and grass, some damp sculpting of mud.
I swore for a moment I saw my daughter's
frayed, pale blue ribbon woven in—my daughter
on her own one thousand miles from us now—while you
made the place from where your beloveds may soar.

Partial List of First Lines

Polishing the morning's stones

Crocheting into songs

Somewhere, before remembering

My mother's one red-haired summer

My father's obsidian reach

Constellations of grief, that light

Compassion, counselled the roses

In Praise of Old Coffee Makers

My mother's Mr. Coffee,
four cups in all, enough
for both of us, gurgling a good morning
from her galley kitchen counter
when I'd come for overnights;

my Yaya's stainless steel pot
on the front burner of her stove
when I was a girl at her table,
the dark liquid popping and burbling up
as if silently singing into the clear glass knob
and waiting to be poured, black with
a dollop of whole milk—nothing fancy
or pressed or flavored, only itself
like a staple of love.

Imagining Heaven

after Paul Zimmer

I am sitting beside Shakespeare
in Gertrude Stein's studio.
We are listening to John Keats
recite an ode.
The mullioned windows are flung open—
brightness unheard of gushes in—
one nightingale perches
on a particular beam of sun.

Just now, Emily D. glides in,
arms linked with the other Emily.
Charlotte follows close behind,
the sequel to *Jane Eyre* in her hands.

Renoir sets up his easel, a cigar
hanging off his lips, while Emerson and Jung
smile from the settee.
Johannes and Clare settle close
on the silk-draped piano bench,
their fingers nearly touching.

Outside, Satchmo and Dizzy
are warming up in the gazebo.
Mozart chats on the lawn with Frida Kahlo.
Just now, Monet arrives
offering a bouquet of water lilies splashed
with water and light—a gift from our Hostess
who is everywhere
though unseen.

Weekend Away

To be immersed, even
briefly, in small pools
and streams of the new—

(though you know you are still
a self with all
edges and fralities)

for these three days—to be lifted
like a gift, shining,
from the box of your life.

Conversing With Keats

200th anniversary celebration, Hampstead.

Waiting for visitors, he stood
in his study at Wentworth Place
and welcomed me in: *Hello Madame.*
I gave him news of a poem:
a most beautiful title he told me.
We conversed of the burgeoning spring
beyond his windows, the nightingale he'd been relishing
at dusk these past days; the inkpot on his desk, and the rustlings
of his pen like tiny creatures of inspiration
as he pins thoughts on paper scraps left laying around.
And when he asked of me, *From where does
your inspiration arrive?* I blurted: *From you of course!*
I swear I caught slivers of light in his eyes
before his gentle modesty translated into a bow, before I floated
away from him and out of the room.

What Did You Do In London, I Was Asked

circled the tombs of the Scots Queen
and the first Elizabeth finally
united in stone,

napped on the grass of Queen
Mary's Garden, as if underwater
with sunlight and hyacinths,

stepped inside the lobby of the Ritz,
down the hushed rose carpeted stairs, I might have heard
the swish of Audrey Hepburn's gown,

sat in the bedroom of John Keats, a spinning
around my heart like a bird—perhaps his nightingale—
arrived from the branches of longing and dream.

Writing At Home With Emily D.

The quiet with a presence
as if stillness were its spine—
a discipline erect
that grants me moments
and words as eternity.

In Early Summer You Start to Understand

what Keats might have meant when
he wrote of the weight in his heart
like a load of immortality,

a mingling of longing, distance
and the nearness of joy, as close
as Adam's fingers to God's in that immense

ceiling Keats never got to see, but surely he suspected it
in the deep hours of June with green lathering over

everything, and the tall stalks of daisies swaying so close
you can almost hear inside their yellow cores;

when the red-edged peonies
can't help but bow under
their weight of impossible beauty.

Religious Moment

On my Yaya's cross-stitched
embroidered tablecloth
in heaven's kitchen:
the dough breathing
in her round porcelain bowl—
a living thing
offering a vision
of golden forms to come.

Studio Sessions

Emily Dickinson Museum

This is a mighty room/within its precincts hopes have played.—E.D.

Two hundred dollars for one hour
may be nothing for the chance
to sit (given one small table and chair)
breathing the air of her room.
Surely some atoms of her being still
linger, though the counterpane
would be new, the lace curtains
pristinely laundered since her touch.

With only pencil and paper (no touching
of the furnishings allowed), how would it be to live
in the aftermath of her? Would she guide
my hand across the modern page?
Could I float along the lost thermals
of her thought? Would ambition keep me
stalled, forgetting how it was
the nobodies she favored.

The Cello

Strings slide in
from somewhere
under,
carve out
the hollows
the deeper
sounds
of our bones.
Once they come—
no escaping
our quiet wounds
that just want to be music now.

Truth, Beauty

Poet friends have cautioned me
about using those words, they
were John Keats' after all, and he
is long dead.
Hasn't the 19th century
gone the way of London fog,
chamber pots,
whalebone corsets?
No one, I was told,
will believe
those words in a poem
with no modern ground
to plant them, ominously perched as they are
on precipices of prayer.

St. Stephens Green After Rain

Dublin

Whoever St. Stephen was,
I bow to him
now for these winding
paths of overarching
leaf and mist
and more leaf, green
so deep
it has rungs,
for these round fountains,
these swans
gliding soundlessly
to the shore of the stream—
ambassadors
of angels too busy for earth,
assigned here
to instruct us in something—
here they come now
seeking one more crust of blessed bread.

Manet's Brushstroke

Raised off the canvas surface
as if swirled by the hand of some
beneficent storm—

you could almost step inside, be held
in the center of whorled
petals and light—the closest

you will ever come to hearing
the beating heart of the rose.

Visitation

I thought I was alone, then
a gentle motor sounded
from a foot away; I turned
to watch her dip into the
heart of the columbine,

before swiftly she changed direction,
bobbing in air
just inches from my face.
I swear she tried to stare me down.

I could not look away, held
my breath, as if to discern
her hushed message—was it something about
the eternal whirring, something about
how the miraculous is true.

Finding My Mother in an Emily Dickinson Poem

found poem

A quietness distilled
as Spring was born to June,
the dusk of breath that drew her
earlier in and then

as imperceptibly as grief
my mother lapsed away
that blue-gold afternoon—

my mother made her light escape
      into the beautiful.

The Cardinal Reminds Me

It sweeps and arcs across my path
almost every day on my walk to the cafe,
under sun or cloud, its red
seems lit from inside, a brightness
bold as the lipstick my mother wore
no matter the day or the time,
no matter how near to the end
she got, even two days before the last—
the young dark-haired nurse applying it
for her while I sat near, my own
lips trembling from fear or hope
I could not tell, I could not separate anything,
not now either—the bright flame of this bird
recalling me to loss, or to joy.

Revelation in Retail

They told me to leave the register;
I wandered over to ribbons,
to replenish all the spools where I could.
At my feet, a box of overstock.
I stood there, struck
by all the hues, announcing
their presence—red like the pith of each rose
in Queen Mary's garden,
silver with a sheen like etched
lightning in late summer.
And the green—oh the green—
the forest I once dream-walked
through and thought I had lost.
And then the ivory, gleaming
like the insides of a shell, or the pearlescent
sky on that morning my daughter
arrived in this world.

In That Moment, A Knowing

It wasn't the proverbial
lightning zag that struck,

nor the small whisper at your ears
or the lightbulb above your head.

It resembled more a last brushstroke
your hand made across the canvas

revealing the scene suddenly
you knew to be true.

Some Notes on an American Impressionist Painting

Philip Leslie Hale

Four girls in a field—
their draping white gowns,
hair rimmed with gold like halos of breath.
To call them cutouts of angels
or simply, angels, would be easy
though they must, in 1892, have been
human girls, for a moment embodied
in glint and shining,
light etched upon light.

Poem on My Daughter's 23rd Birthday

That morning the December sky sifted
white quiet over everything,
how terrified I was to push across the threshold
of the known.
If someone had asked, I might have pleaded to stay
suspended in that hammock
between worlds, swaying
on the cusp,
before being thrust into the strange and raw air
expanding with tiny cries and my life,
that gift, never just mine again.

Partial Syllabus of Red

Oh longest wavelength of all visible light,
cochineal bugs crushed fine
by the early Aztecs,

vermilion glazed with egg yolks for medieval manuscripts,
rose madder first made from the root
of *Rubia tinctorum* in Greece.

Cadmium red and burgundy,
carmine, crimson and Terra Rosa,
Mars the red planet.

The Indian goddess of abundance and beauty Lashkmi
wore it. The Chinese named ruby for long life.
Ruby slippers and matador caps,

early physicians in red robes to signify their healing work,
sienna used by cave painters of Lauscaux. Cinnabar
and scarlet, Helios red,

the cardinal birds' red flapping at the windowpane
after a loved one's passing—bright messengers arrived
from the other side of love.

On the Anniversary of My Mother's Passing

This summer day the clouds
are hues of moonstone and the insides
of abalone shells,

a slate blue and pale coral pink of a sky
where the sun might be setting or
it might be rising, you're not sure which,

the way you could say
the body is dying,
or the spirit is waking up.

Just Born

for Madeline Olive

Swathed in flannel, she mewled
a little in my arms which seemed to register
almost no weight at all.
The tiny crescent moons of her fingernails
rose in the air where she'd been
so suddenly gathered

as if to say: hmmm, so this
is the world of air
and breath; give me time
to adapt to your ways,
I don't have voice to tell you yet
all that I know.

Final Poem for an Estranged Friend

for S.

My last dream had me chasing you
along some narrow stone path rising and twisting
on a Greek island mountainside
while I screamed at you to finally believe
I had not wronged you. Still,
you kept your righteous gait.

I awoke exhausted from all
my efforts, recent and past,
decided I must rest.
I remembered, in the dream,
in the darkness beside me lay the Mediterranean
sea of my ancestors, lapis and deep
and dazzling by daylight—
water that knew my innocence.

The Woman in the Van Gogh Painting

She may be skimming the air
in her pale white gown,
around her the flowers may
or may not have butterflies
as petals, and her hair may
or may not be ochre waves escaped
from a sun-torched ocean somewhere beyond
the distance, and her hands,
oh her hands, where do they
begin, where do they end
though there is no end

Last Conversation With My Friend

For Eric

though of course I did not know it
when he rose from the sofa where
he'd been dozing (the tumor plunging
deeper into his brain each day),
the same gladness to see me on his face
as ever, a quick hug, with me holding
a plate of brownies in one hand—
triple chip Ghiradelli I announced as
he beamed and led me to the kitchen counter
to lay it down, thanking me again
and again, and when I opened the screen door
to leave, I felt the wake of his goodness
behind me and everywhere.

Visiting the Hospice

Call it heaven already—
air of ochre light, art on the walls—
a mosaiced Balinese dancer, a cathedral of orchids.
I glimpse siderooms filled with books,
leather sofas to sink inside, windows
with green views of paths winding
somewhere I cannot see.
Along the spacious hallways,
no one hurries.
Each person who greets me
carries a stillness I long to keep.
My friend sleeps most of the day now;
at the door of his room, I pause,
knowing the safety of his passage.

Where to Find Them

If a scent had wings—whisking past you.

Sunk in the haymows of your longing,

Beyond the last camera roll,

Stitched inside the heart's silk repository,

Inside the sealed envelopes of this world—

Within the marrow of every summer
    there ever was or will be.

Being Spider

Oh this morning
that tightrope of shine

strung between
chair frame and railing ledge;

I watched it there, bobbing with light—
fragile, persistent, daring—

unafraid of anything
that may pass to break it.

Essential Gratitude

Sometimes, it just stuns you
like an arrow flung from some angel's wing.
Sometimes it hastily scribbles
a list in the air: black coffee,
thick new books,
your pillow's cool underside,
the quirky family you married into.

It is content with so little really;
even the ink of your pen along
the watery lines of your dimestore notebook
could be a swiftly moving prayer.

All Travel Plans Cancelled

And so Connemara will be
conjured in my mind, our first
Irish journey four summers ago when
we drove through light-shot deep greening
and mist, wildness gentle and unscathed,
peats bogs and mountains and lashings of rain,
the landscape turning to song in our mouths
its very syllables unrolling to now.

Daughter, Home

Pandemic 2020

Oh I wish for the irrational—
to have her here always,
not two thousand miles away where
her life is after college.
My heart croons a little to hear
her laughter from two floors away, when
I see the dinner table set for three and not two,
the dishwasher loaded with extra bowls
and flatware; when I have to remember
to buy the 1% not the skim milk this time;
when she asks can I please fry up some eggs
over-easy because she says she can never get them
just right; even when I blow it and the yolk breaks
and spills its bright gold all over the pan, to hear her say:
Thanks Mom, that is just fine, this is so good.

In the Last Days of July, My Father

Already ten days in ICU,
my father opened his eyes and talked,
more than nonsense this time, he said
our names and teased us
like a man on the verge
of reunion with time.

For two days he gave us
the gift of relief, the heart's
blessed respite.
We did not yet understand he too
needed a rest on his journey—

though he paused along the way
to take us in once more.

June Memoriam

The green warm
season has come
round, the months
of leavings, aged
and newer: my mother,
my father,
my baby uncle gone long
before I was here,
all returned
now in the deep
emerald dreaming, shadows
and flickering light—time
has woven a nest for loss.

Partial Syllabus of Yellow

Bright yellow Helios
galloping a chariot across mythic skies

cadmium and chrome yellow,
warm Naples yellow gleaned from the volcanic

earth of the ancients.
Lemon yellow, golden ochre

and 17th century gamboge from the resin
of the *Garcina hanburyi tree.*

Ground gold for the sacred pages,
powdered gold as watercolor to illuminate.

The first artists of yellow adorning cave walls
of Lauscaux and Altamira—eons before

Van Gogh and his Arles yellow,
his cornfields, peasants and cafes, his sunflowers

and more sunflowers, and yellow rooms
endlessly burning with his light.

Dreams, Again

Layered and washed
one over another flowing fast

scenes spooling off the mind
and impossible to hold

rising as I must, back
to the arid world—relief

and disappointment both,
I swear there were gems

in there somewhere—
abalone shine of my mother's voice—

lost again, now back
into the deep fathoms.

The Sisters

Frank Weston Benson, American Impressionist

If children were boats
and air were water,

if the fabric of dresses were opal light,
grasses the wind turned gold,

if a heaven freed the gaze to see
the sisters here

When Beginning the Poem

may there be a listening
rather than a making

curiosity over expectation,

lightness and ease,
no straining
toward some glut of air.

May you step aside
like a watcher at the meadow's edge
as the doe
finds her way to the center.

Poem On What Would Have Been My Mother's 90th Birthday

In less than a second, it appeared—
not a flash exactly, more like

a snapshot that fit
in the frame of my chest:

    my heart had a throne—
she sat there

reigning over everything.

Visiting the Graves

They chose simplicity in small bronze
plaques set into the earth,
raised letters for their names:
my mother, her sister, her mother
and father, her baby brother—oldest
and most burnished: 1935-1939.
My feet sink into grass sodden
from last night's storm. The air is thick
with song—cicadas strumming in tall oaks,
their insistence of late summer leaving.
The marigold bed my grandmother wanted
gleams with orange and ochre yellow,
and I think of Van Gogh, his words
to brother Theo: *Even in pressing darkness,*
There is a sun.

My Grandmother's First Name For Me

Years after her death, I go searching for her
at the summer Greek festival
where the old women
sell the *diples* and *baklava,*
the rings of *koulouria* in the dusky,
cool basement of the church.
Her friend Dina is nearing 100;
with mottled skin, hands that quiver
when she gives me
the plate of sweets.
Her eyes sheen with memory
of the Old Country,
of my grandmother

when I remind her who I am:
Aristea's granddaughter,
and this is Lexi, I say of my daughter
wriggling free in my arms.

Dina pats my cheek—
Koukla
she says to my child
as something deep in my body
bows to its source.

When A Certain Word Comes to You

This morning it was *fluency,*
the title of a poem I found in a book
I laid aside so I could write this down and find
myself inside generous syllables rippling along
waters leading somewhere hopeful I am sure
like a readiness of well-being or forgiveness, and just now
the face of the woman who had wronged me bitterly
came to my mind and in place of my common anger
this time I felt only the residue of her own wounding
and my heart, its jagged edges closer to smooth.

Of Prayer Now

After cocooning
myself in my comforter
before sleep comes,

I lay with eyes open
in the dark. One by one
I conjure them all,
finding again
their magnanimous, smiling faces—
my queue of beloveds,
returned. This

is the way of prayer now—
to remember Love in all
its past and present forms.

Always Believe Something Wonderful Is About To Happen

That just when I look up—a ruby-throated angel
will alight on my backyard petunias,

that the breaking morning headline will read:
"Vaccine trials crowned a success, distribution soon to follow"

that I will open my Inbox to find the subject line
"Congratulations," and it won't be spam

and the momentary breeze will suddenly bring me
the long-ago scents of my father's chapstick, and

the laundry tin my mother kept in her kitchen cupboard—
accruals of cinnamon, old smoke,
and all the consolations of anise.

Gratitude on a Winter Morning

For my husband hauling the Green machine up
three flights of stairs to scrub away the mold
discovered behind my bookcase;

for the hostess at my neighborhood cafe who
left her perch to deliver to my tucked-away table
the small fatfree cappucino while I bent

over my notebook, thinking how the December air
today is forecast to be nineteen degrees warmer than
yesterday which feels like the tiniest whisper of summer,

a hint of a premonition: warmth and promise, even
to murmur the word *summer* right now makes me remember
how every moment we are on our way there.

About the Author

Andrea Potos is the author of nine poetry collections, including *Mothershell* (Kelsay Books), *A Stone to Carry Home* (Salmon Poetry,), *Arrows of Light* (Iris Press), *An Ink Like Early Twilight* (Salmon Poetry), *We Lit the Lamps Ourselves* (Salmon Poetry) and *Yaya's Cloth* (Iris Press). Several of her books received Outstanding Achievement Awards in Poetry from the Wisconsin Library Association. She received the William Stafford Prize in Poetry from *Rosebud* Magazine, and the James Hearst Poetry Prize from the *North American Review*. Her poems have been featured widely in print and online, including *Spirituality & Health Magazine, gratefulness.org, Verse Daily, One Art, Your Daily Poem, Women Artist's Datebook (*Syracuse Cultural Workers), *Poetry East, Cave Wall, Women's Review of Books, Atlanta Review, Southern Poetry Review, Poem, Sou'wester, Poetry Ireland Review, Literary Mama, Mom Egg Review, Sunlight Press,* and many others, including *How to Love the World: Poems of Gratitude and Hope* (Storey Publishing), *I Feel A Little Jumpy Around You* (Simon & Schuster), and *Claiming the Spirit Within* (Beacon Press). Andrea worked for many years as a bookseller in independent bookstores. She lives in Madison, Wisconsin.

Kelsaybooks.com

Made in the USA
Columbia, SC
24 July 2022

63948217R00043